bootees

lime

nails

leaf

scuba diver

DK
A DK PUBLISHING BOOK
www.dk.com

for Kyle and Jack

Editor Lara Tankel Holtz
Art Editor Helen Melville
U.S. Editor Camela Decaire
Editorial Assistant Jennifer Siklós
Designer Anna Benckert
Picture Researcher Sam Ruston
Production Simon Shelmerdine
Managing Editor Sheila Hanly

Illustrations by Lisa Flather and C. David Gillingwater
Photography by Dave King, Gary Ombler, Tim Ridley,
Paul Bricknell, Steve Gorton, Stephen Oliver, ,
Philip Gatward, Steve Shott, Kit Houghton, Karl Shone,
Kim Taylor, Jane Burton, Frank Greenaway, Bill Ling
Neil Fletcher, Peter Chadwick, Cyril Laubscher,
Gregory Scott, David Murray, Alex Wilson,
Gordon Clayton, Jon Bouchier, Nick Paratt,
Geoff Brightling, Clive Streeter, Jo Foord.

First American Edition, 1996
6 8 10 9 7 5
Published in the United States by
DK Publishing, Inc., 95 Madison Avenue,
New York, New York 10016

Photography (jaguar on page 30)
copyright © 1991 Philip Dowell.
Photography (alligator, gray wolf on page 30; crowned
crane on page 34) copyright © 1991 Jerry Young.
Photography (mouse on page 5, page 29)
copyright © 1991 Barrie Watts.

Published in Great Britain by Dorling Kindersley Limited.
Distributed by Houghton Mifflin Company, Boston.

A CIP catalog record is available from the Library of Congress.
ISBN 0-7894-0998-4
Color reproduction by Colourscan , Singapore
Printed and bound in Spain by Artes Gráficas Toledo, S.A.U.
D.L. TO: 1537 - 1999

baker

broccoli

milk

soft toy

apple

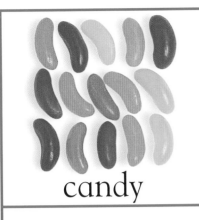

candy

crow

baby

kite

waitress

MY
BIG BOOK
OF
EVERYTHING

Roger Priddy

DK

mail carrier

orange

mouse

paint set

bulldozer

porcupine

waving

bear

sipper cup

firefighter

Contents

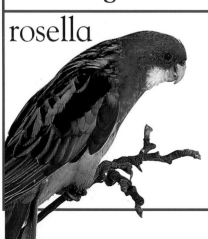
rosella

gloves

cookies

tulips

cement mixer

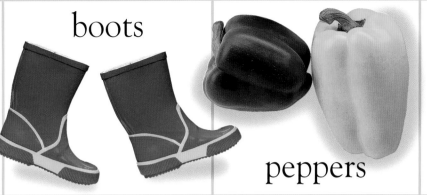

boots

peppers

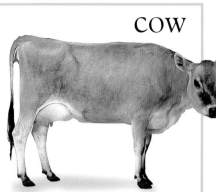

cow

ballerina

carrots

fish

sweater

airplane

Around the home

lamp

rug

sipper cup

tea kettle

table

spoon

brush

chair

vase

book

soaps

bath

cushion

telephone

clothespins

fork

laundry

Around the home

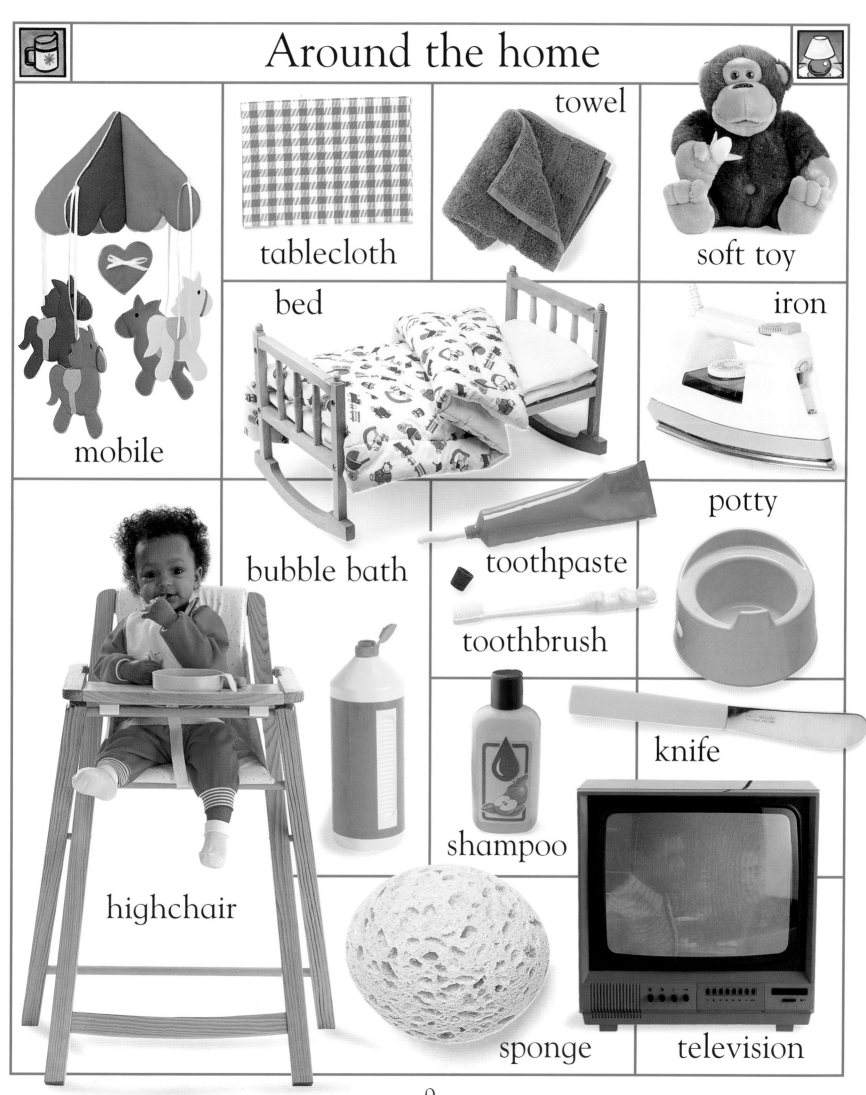

mobile

tablecloth

towel

soft toy

bed

iron

bubble bath

toothpaste

toothbrush

potty

highchair

shampoo

knife

sponge

television

9

Clothes

jeans

sweater

tights

hat

bootees

diaper

swimsuit

slippers

shoes

T-shirt

overalls

scarf and gloves

coat

sleeper

Clothes

cardigan

bib

sweatsuit

shorts

robe

dress

underwear

pajamas

snowsuit

socks

boots

pants

Toys and games

swinging

airplane

tractor

pencils

balls

play stove

puzzle

doll

dress-up

boat

paint set

roller skates

Toys and games

painting

kite

spinning top

crayons

teddy bear

car

push toy

soldiers

soft blocks

pail and shovel

stacking rings

rattle

train set

Cooking and baking

measuring cups

cutting board

brown sugar

beans

pitcher

wooden spoon

apron

wok

rolling pin

cookie cutters

mixing bowl

milk

cooling rack

Cooking and baking

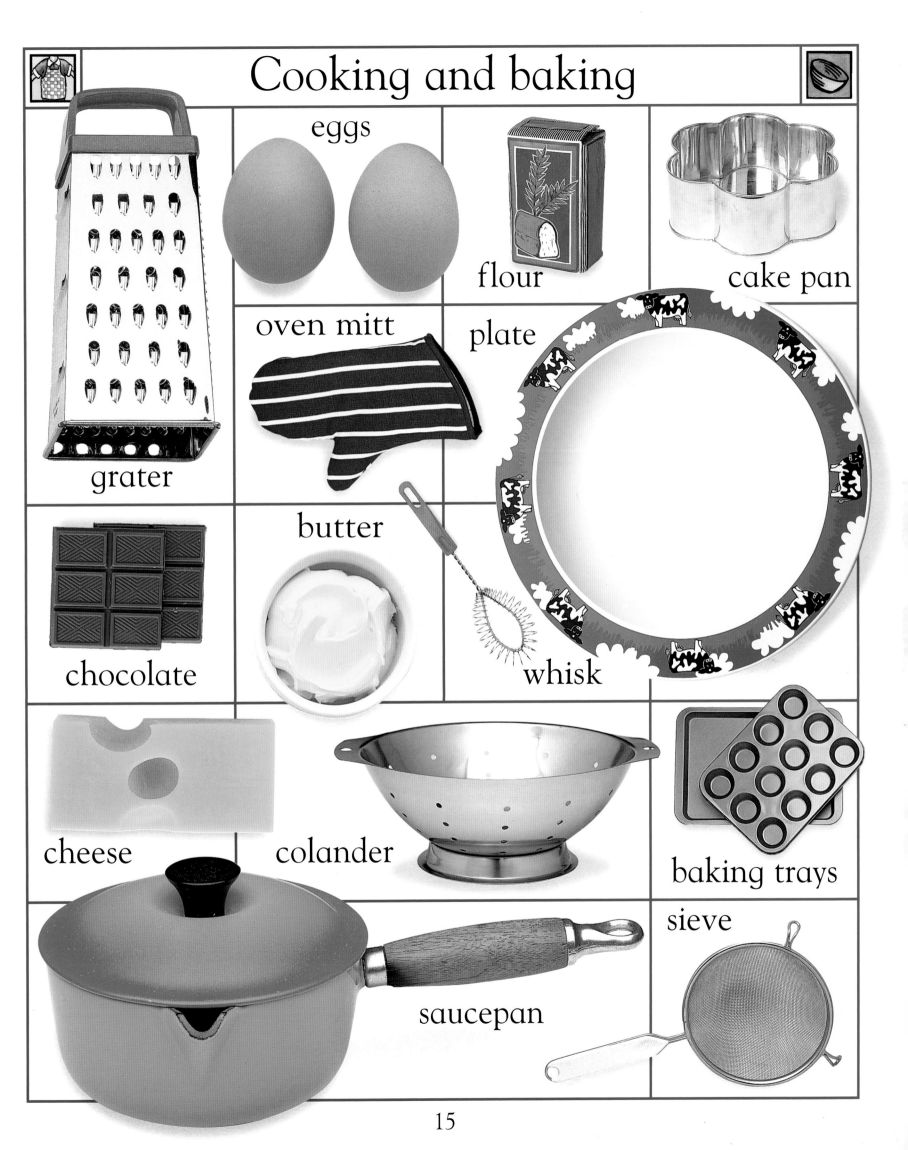

grater

eggs

flour

cake pan

oven mitt

plate

butter

chocolate

whisk

cheese

colander

baking trays

sieve

saucepan

Food to eat

fruit pie

muffins

hot chocolate

sandwiches

chicken

yogurt

pizza

stew

milkshakes

cookies

cereal

cake

orange juice

candy

Food to eat

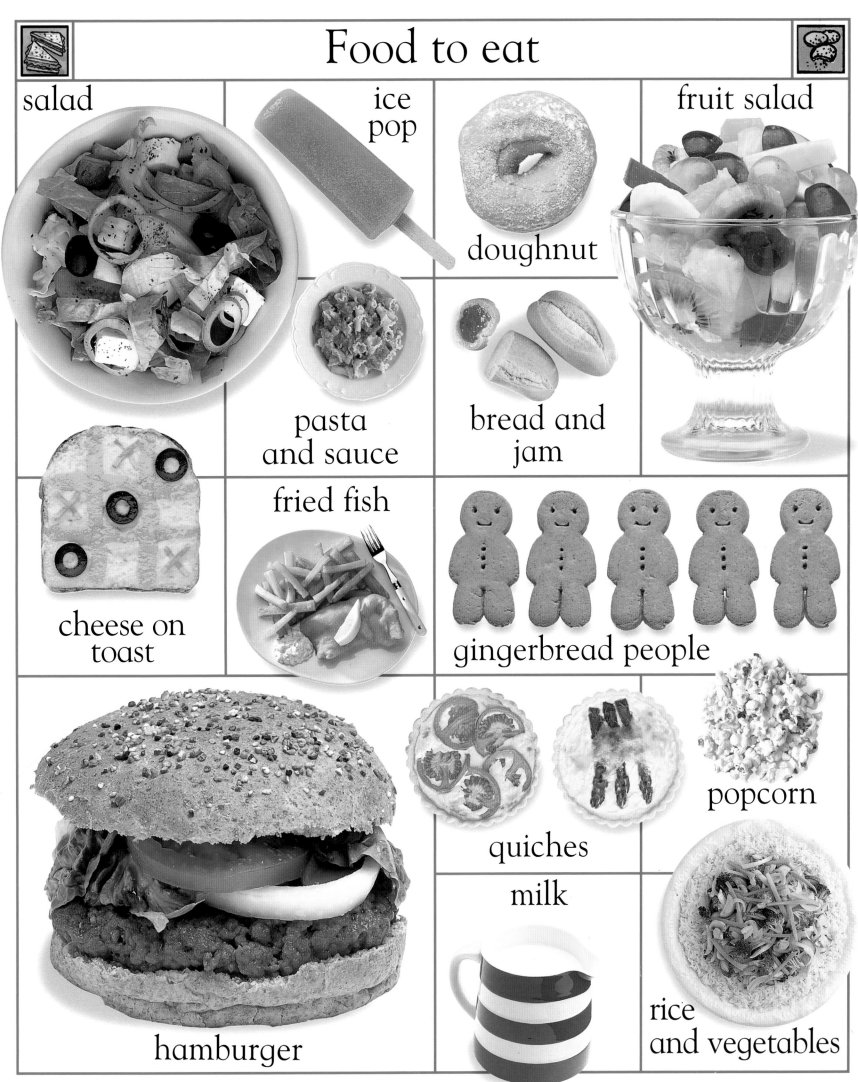

salad

ice pop

doughnut

fruit salad

pasta and sauce

bread and jam

cheese on toast

fried fish

gingerbread people

hamburger

quiches

milk

popcorn

rice and vegetables

Fruit

pear

peaches

cherries

lime

mango

pineapple

lemons

plums

raspberries

orange

apple

bananas

grapes

strawberries

melon

18

Vegetables

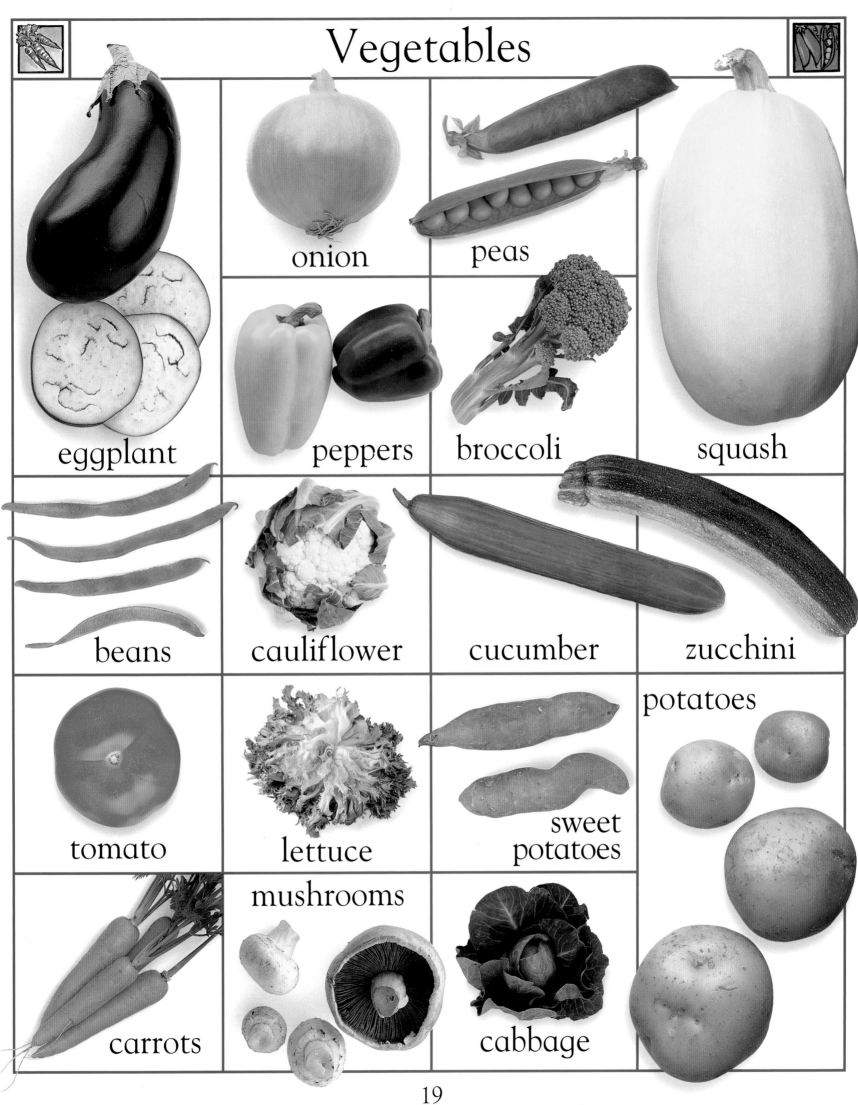

eggplant

onion

peas

squash

peppers

broccoli

beans

cauliflower

cucumber

zucchini

potatoes

tomato

lettuce

sweet potatoes

mushrooms

carrots

cabbage

In the workshop

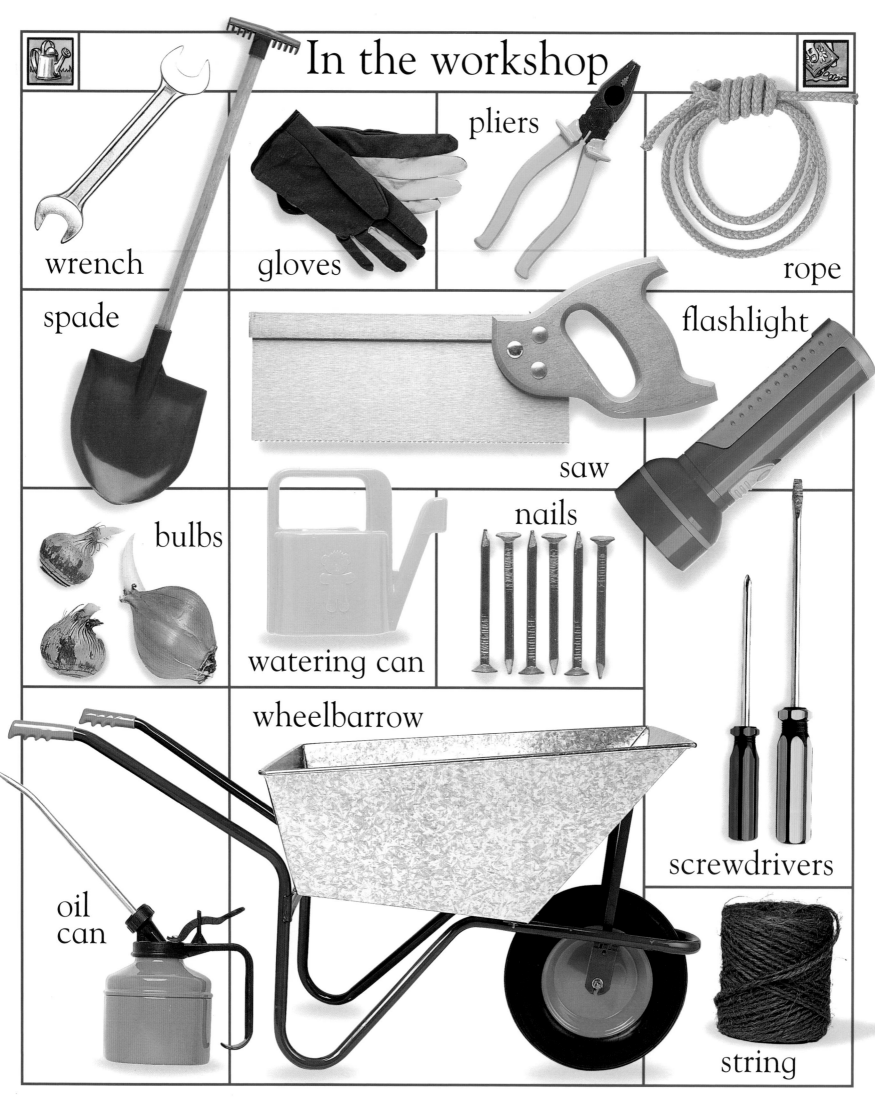

wrench

gloves

pliers

rope

spade

saw

flashlight

bulbs

watering can

nails

wheelbarrow

screwdrivers

oil can

string

In the workshop

drill

screws

paintbrush

plant pots

ladder

hose

fork

bicycle

mallet

spider

hammer

trowel

lawnmower

seeds

toolbox

Flowers, trees, and plants

daffodils

cactus

poppies

olive tree

crocuses

orchids

water lily

iris

fuchsias

red-hot pokers

daisies

willow tree

magnolias

redwood tree

ferns

cornflower

Flowers, trees, and plants

sunflower

pine tree

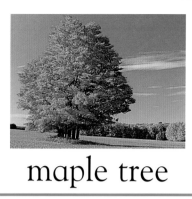
maple tree

thistle

primroses

rose

holly

carnation

oak tree

buttercup

tulips
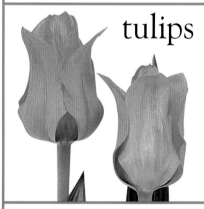

pansy

lily

foxgloves

snowdrops

calendulas

23

Weather

wind

rain

blizzard

sun

icicles

mist

fog

tornado

snow

lightning

storm clouds

Seasons and time

spring

summer

fall

winter

morning

afternoon

evening

nighttime

On the farm

goat

fields

combine harvester

orchard

horse

tea picking

rubber trees

hen

potato harvest

farmhouse

cotton harvest

straw bales

On the farm

goose

rice fields

wheat field

grape vines

cow

farmyard

tractor

field of sunflowers

pig

sheep herding

turkey

In the countryside

tree seeds

wasp

dragonfly

ducks on a pond

ladybug

bee

stream

leaves

bridge

nest

berries

In the countryside

caterpillar

bark

butterfly

toadstools

country lane

earthworms

pinecones

hillside

snail

feathers

mouse

footprints

meadow

Big animals

lion

zebra

wildebeests

tiger

polar bear

wolf

hippopotamuses

alligator

jaguar

cobra

panther

stag and deer

30

Big animals

rhinoceros

kangaroo

giraffe

panda

herd of elephants

walrus

bear

camel

puma

gorilla

Small animals

fox

rat

chameleon

koala

porcupine

raccoon

opossum

tortoise

squirrel

snake

pig

monkey

bush baby

frog

penguin

rabbit

lizard

Baby animals

bear cub

caiman

duckling

chicks

ostrich chick

foal

lambs

tiger cubs

cygnet

joey

calf

orangutan

puppies

kitten

elephant

fox cubs

kid

33

Birds

galah

albatross

buzzard

falcon

blackbird

peacock

goldfinch

pigeon

hornbill

budgerigar

kookaburra

swan

kestrel

toucan

crane

heron

Birds

parakeet

crow

terns

rosella

cuckoo

cockatoo

dove

gannets

canary

puffins

vulture

parrot

bald eagle

flamingos

pelican

starling

blimp

glider

helicopter

microlight

space shuttle

flock of birds

jumbo jet

moon

rainbow

small aircraft

In the sky

biplane

hot-air balloon

clouds

executive jet

sun

Concorde

G-PITZ

stunt plane

sky divers

stars

kites

parachutist

jet plane

In the sea

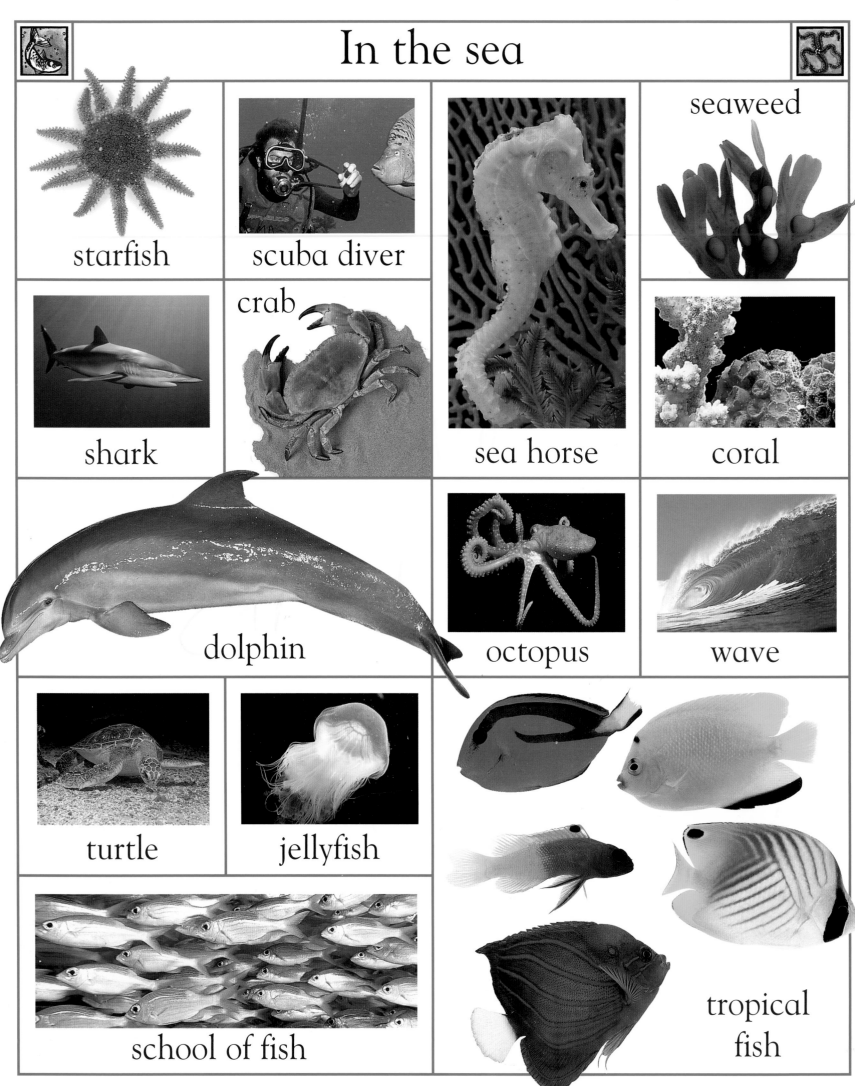

starfish

scuba diver

seaweed

shark

crab

sea horse

coral

dolphin

octopus

wave

turtle

jellyfish

school of fish

tropical
fish

38

cliffs

harbor

shells

fishing trawler

sailboats

cargo ship

surfer

lighthouse

ocean liner

beach

powerboat

junk

pebbles

island

Noises

ooo - oooo ooo ooo
ambulance

crrunch crunch
leaves

drum
bang bang bang
(baby playing drum)

brring brring bring brring
alarm clock

baby
whaaaah

chop chop chop chop chop chop chop chop
helicopter

beeeeeeeeeep
cars

singer
la la la la la la la la

rrrrrrrrrr rrrrrrrrrr
blender

whizz pop bang whizz whooo
fireworks

splish splash
bathing

scissors
snip snip snip

40

sheep

baaaa
baaa

ribbit ribbit
ribbit
ribbit

frog

oink
oink

moooo

cow

dog

whooo whooo

woof
woof
woof

knock
knock
knock
knock
knock
knock
knock

pig

rrooaarr

owl

bear

grrrowlli

woodpecker.

lion

ee ee
eee
ee
eee

monkeys

bee

buzzz buzzz
buzzz

donkey ee-aw
ee-aaw

cat

meeoOOoow

mouse

squeak squeak squeak

In the city

 cyclist

opera house

park

monorail

tow truck

traffic jam

office buildings

traffic lights

skating rink

waterfront

city sidewalk

motorcycle

train station

In the city

fire engine

marina

city lights

café

skyscrapers

truck

market

streetcar

police car

roadworks

water taxi

car

building site

castle

apartments

cabin

windmill

stadium

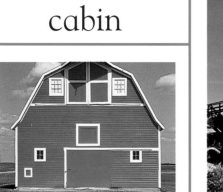
barn

igloo

pyramids

skyscraper

bungalow

hut

tepee

house on stilts

pagoda

Building machines

excavator

truck loader crane

cement mixer

dump truck

forklift

roller

bulldozer

backhoe loader

music store

shopping carts

candy shop

farmers' market

hardware store

shopping mall

supermarket

clothing store

toy store

bookstore

bakery

florist

shoe store

bike shop

fruit stand

fishmonger

magazine stand

checkout

delicatessen

nursery

Jobs people do

waitress

surgeon

builder

chef

mail carrier

teacher

painter

firefighter

mechanic

tennis player

police officer

waiter

Jobs people do

ballerina

nurse's aide

fisherman

sailor

trash collector

scuba diver

baker

soldier

gardener

scientist

pilot

musician

Me and my body

girl

boy

baby

mouth

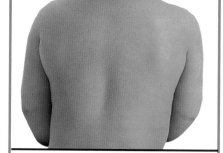

back

eyelashes

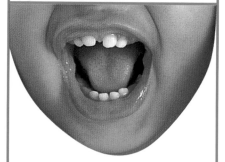

teeth

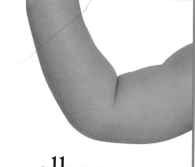

elbow

Me and my body

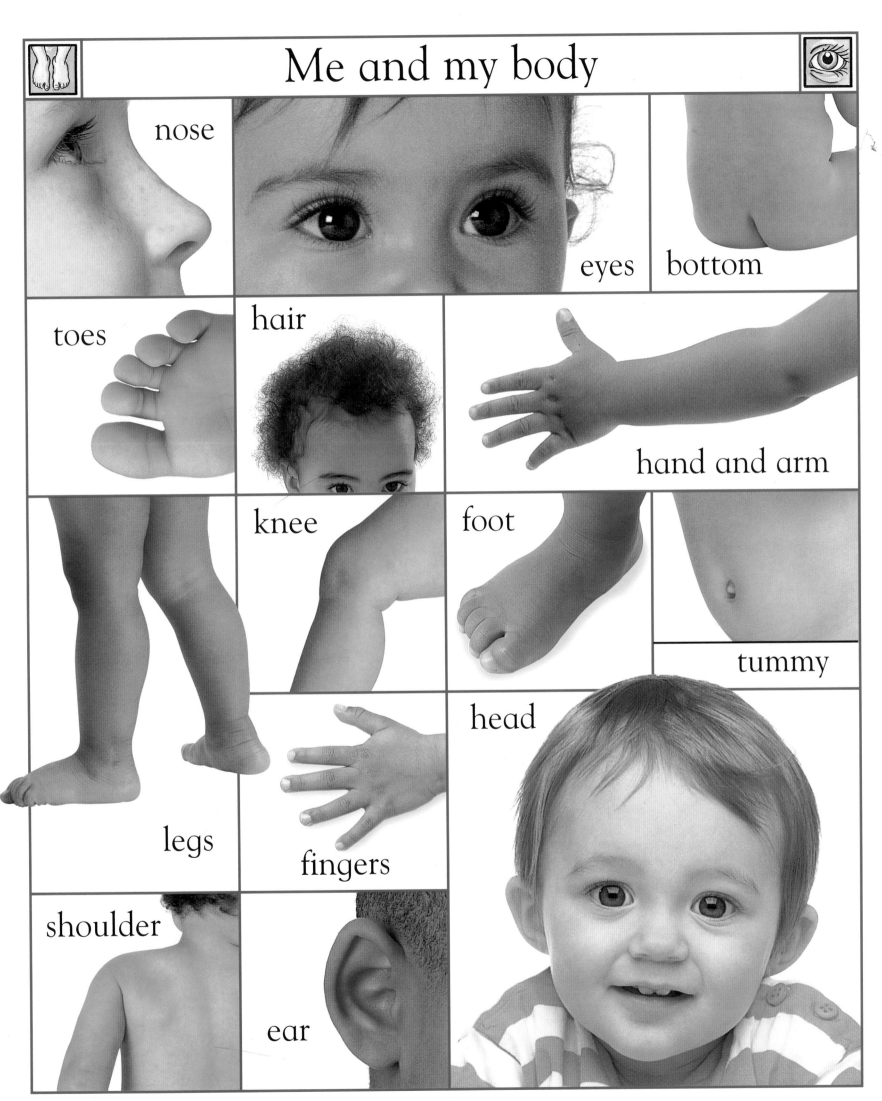

nose

eyes

bottom

toes

hair

hand and arm

knee

foot

tummy

legs

fingers

head

shoulder

ear

Things we do

crying

touching

pushing

walking

carrying

eating

drinking

crawling

yawning

waving

throwing

clapping

52

Things we do

looking

playing

sleeping

picking up

running

smiling

pointing

dancing

hiding

talking

undressing

laughing

Shapes and patterns

What shapes and patterns can you find on this page?

 square

 circle

triangle

 star

 rectangle

 diamond

kite

starfish

windows

moon

sand

hang-glider

hat

dome

buildings

herd of zebras

Colors

white clouds in a blue sky

pink blossoms

silver tower

orange leaves

brown soil

red poppies

gold temple

yellow sunflowers

gray elephant

purple
lavender

green grass

Counting

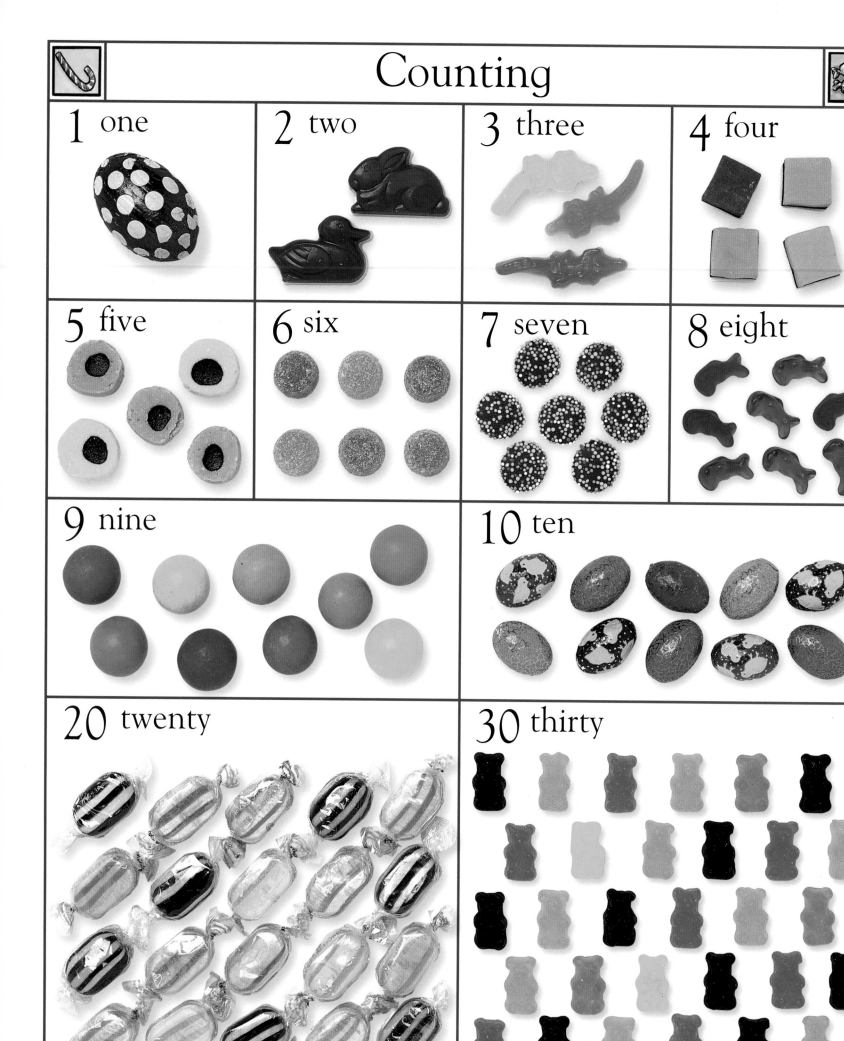

1 one

2 two

3 three

4 four

5 five

6 six

7 seven

8 eight

9 nine

10 ten

20 twenty

30 thirty

50 fifty

100 one hundred

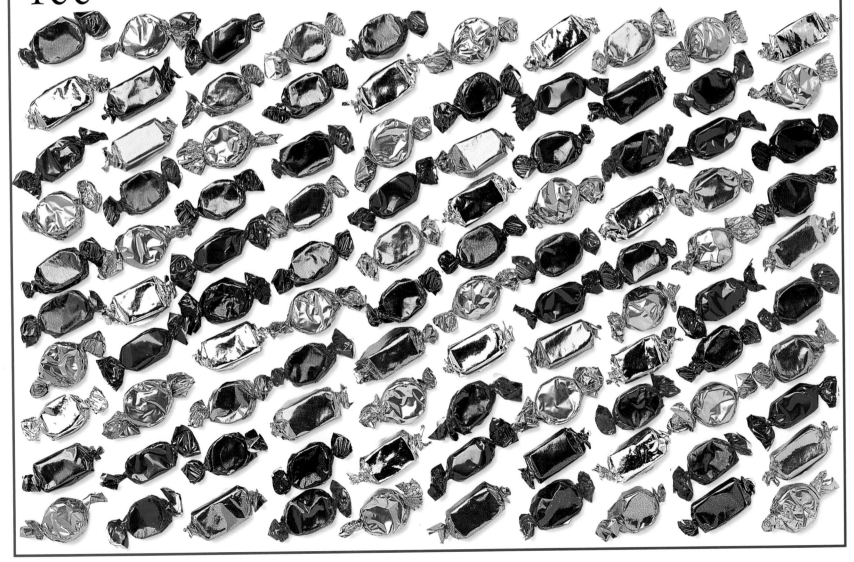

hills

sandy desert

mountain

lake

waterfall

iceberg

volcano

woodland

valley

Around the world

swamp

river

canyon

grassland

geyser

rocky desert

rain forest

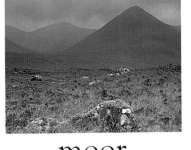

moor

Index

Acknowledgments

The publisher would like to thank the following for their kind permission to reproduce the photographs:

t=top c=center a=above b=below l=left r=right

Bruce Coleman Ltd.: 28crb, 59br, Atlantide 42bcl, David Austen 26bc, Jen & Des Bartlet 35bl, Erik Bjurstrom 25bl, Nigel Blake 55bl, Stephen Bond 55ca, Jane Burton 38tcr, Alain Compost 54cr, Eric Crichton 22bl, Gerald Cubit 58cl, Peter Davey 30tr, Jack Dermid 23tcl, P. Evans 29bc, Jeff Foott Productions 59cr, Michael Freeman 42cb, Francisco Futil 23c, Clive Hicks 39bl, Gordon Langsbury 35cl, Paul Mortimer 22crb, Flip de Nooyer 35cra, Dennis Orchard 44tl, Mary Plage 22tcl, Allan G. Potts 35t, 36cr, Fritz Prenzel 59bl, Hans Reinhard 25tl, 32cra, 55cr, front cover crb, back cover crb, Jeffrey L Rotman 38c, John Shaw 23tcr, 55cla, Kim Taylor 29tc, Norman Tomalin 43cla; *Philip Dowell:* 30clb, 31tr, front cover bl, cla, back cover cra; *Galaxy Picture Library:* 36cb; *Robert Harding Picture Library:* 24rc, 37cl, bl, 46bl, 47ca, br; *The Image Bank:* 44cb, Walter Bibikow 43clb, Steve Bronstein 24cr, A. Caufield 42tl, Andy Caulfield 40br, Alain Choisnet 46tcr, Grant V. Faint 42cr, John P Kelly 42clb, Don & Liysa King 38cr, Don Klumpp 22tr, David Maenza 44cl, Novosti Press 44bcl, Ombreski 46bc, Jean Pierre Pieuchot 27cr, Magnus Rietz 44cla, Marc Romanelli 37tc, Bernard Roussel 27clb, Jeff Spielman 46br, Harald Sund 39tc, Joe Szkodzinski 44ca, Vic Verlinden 38tcl, Terry Williams 46tl, Williamson/ Edwards 36tr, Yellow Dogs Prods. 40tl; *Frank Lane Picture Agency:* Silvestris 24tcr; *Natural History Photographic Agency:* Agence Nature 38cra, ANT 34tc, B. Jones & M. Shimlock front cover cl, back cover cl, Trevor McDonald 38clb, Michael Morcombe 34cr; *Pictor International Ltd.:* 24crb, tr, 25cr, 36crb; *Pictures Colour Library:* Willi Arand - Halga Lade Fotoagenture 37crb; *Planet Earth Pictures:* Sean Avery 30cl, Doug Perrine 38cla; *Tony Stone Images:* 30br, 39cl, 42br, 44bl, br, front cover bc, Glen Allison 39bc, Doug Armand 43br, 46cl, David Austen 44crb, James Balog 44c, Oliver Benn 43tc, Paul Berger 37tr, Ken Biggs 54cra, cl, front cover tl, back cover tl, Rob Bondrean 25tr, Gary Braasch 59bc, Marcus Brooke 44tc, Tim Brown 24ca, Michael Busselle 55bc, 58cb, John Callahan 39tc, John Chard 55tl, Paul Chesley 58br, Daniel J. Cox 35crb, Phil Degginger 26cla, Geoff Dore 39tl, Wayne Eastep 42cl, John Edwards 44tr, 58cr, Shaun Egan 26cb, Chad Ehlers 39cr, 59tr, John Elk 42c, Jake Evans 25br, David R. Frazier 26c, tc, John & Eliza Forder 25cl, Jane Gifford 29ca, Janet Gill 55tc, Bruce Hands 43cr, 58bc, Chris Harvey 59cl, Arnulf Husmo 39tr, Chuck Keeler 47cr, Peter Lamberti 37clb, Tom Mackie 55cl, James Martin 24cl, Murkay & Associates 26br, Ian Murphy 44bcr, Michael Orton 29tr, Richard Passmore 39tc, Mark Peterson 37cla, Colin Prior 39clb, Ed Pritchard 40cl, James Randklev 55br, Donovan Reese 27tc, Schafer & Hill 33cl, Mark Segal 46cr, Hugh Sitton 26cra, 44cr, Stephen Studd 27tr, David Sutherland 24cl, Rob Talbot front cover br, Oli Tennent 39crb, Larry Ulrich 28cr, 59tl, Greg Vaughn 58bl, Mark Wagner 36cl, Charlie Waite 24br, Jeremy Walker 25clb, John Warden 28cla, Denis Waugh 27br, Kim Wersterskov 37cb, Stuart Westmorland 38bl, Art Wolfe 31c, 54br, David Woodfall 29cl; *Trip Photographic Library:* H Rogers 42tr, B Turner 43cr; *Barrie Watts* 29clb; *Zefa Pictures:* 22cl, 24tl, 26cl, 27bc, 27cl, 29br, 43ca, cl, 46cb, 46tcl, tr, 47rl, bl, c, 54bc, bl, 55tr, 58tl, 58tc, tr, ca, 59tc, front cover ca, B. Binzen 25crb, B. Berenholtz 43tr, Bontin 47cl, Connie Coleman 42rt, S. Elmore 46cra, Fiala 39br, Gerolf Kalt 54c, G. Mabbs 24bl, Dr. Mueller 54cla, Raga 42bcr, Rosenfeld 47tc, Stockmarket 36tl, 37ca, Andrea Strasmann 47tr, Dr. P Thiele 55cra.

Every effort has been made to trace the copyright holders. DK apologizes for any unintentional omissions and would be pleased, in such cases, to add an acknowledgment in future editions.